RSPB first book of

flowers

Anita Ganeri and David Chandler

A & C

Published 2011 by A&C Black Publishers Limited
36 Soho Square, London W1D 3QY
www.acblack.com

ISBN: 978-1-4081-3717-8

Printed and bound in China by WKT.

A&C Black uses paper produced from elemental
chlorine-free pulp, harvested from managed
sustainable forests.

Contents

Flowers

Flowers are everywhere! When you're out and about, you might have seen bright yellow buttercups or big red poppies.

This book will help you name lots of the wild flowers you can see around you, and tell you where they like to grow. See which ones you can spot. Have a good look at them. But please don't pick them. Leave them where they are. Then other people will be able to enjoy the wild flowers too.

At the back of this book is a Spotter's Guide to help you remember the wild flowers you spot. You could also write down the flowers you see, or draw them.

Happy flower hunting!

Buttercup

Buttercups have shiny, yellow flowers.
Look for them in grassy places.
Sometimes, there are so many of them
they can make whole fields look yellow!

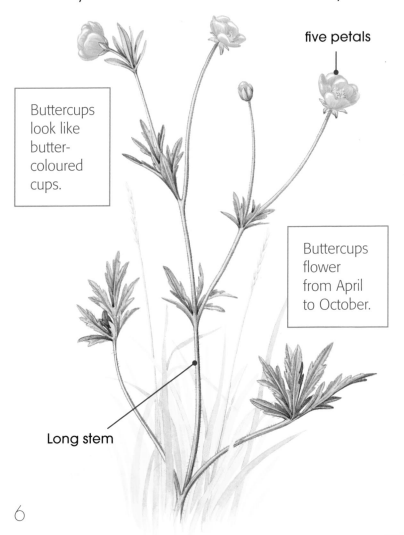

five petals

Buttercups
look like
butter-
coloured
cups.

Buttercups
flower
from April
to October.

Long stem

Lesser celandine

Lesser celandines are bright yellow but have more petals than the buttercup. You can see them in meadows and woods, and on grassy banks.

Lesser celandines flower from February to May.

They grow in the shade. They open when the sun comes out and close when it goes in.

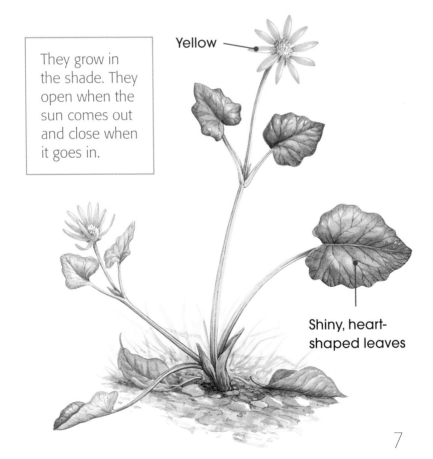

Yellow

Shiny, heart-shaped leaves

Cowslip

Look for cowslips in April and May. You can find them in grassy places and woods. They have bunches of yellow flowers on tall stems.

The name 'cowslip' comes from an old word for cow poo!

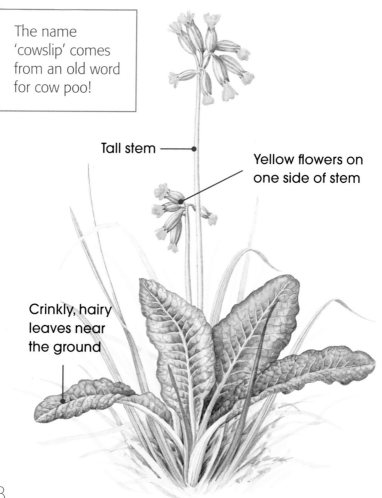

Tall stem

Yellow flowers on one side of stem

Crinkly, hairy leaves near the ground

Primrose

Primroses and cowslips look very similar. However, primroses only grow one flower on each stem. You might see them in woods, hedges and fields.

Primroses bloom very early in the year. You will see them from January to June.

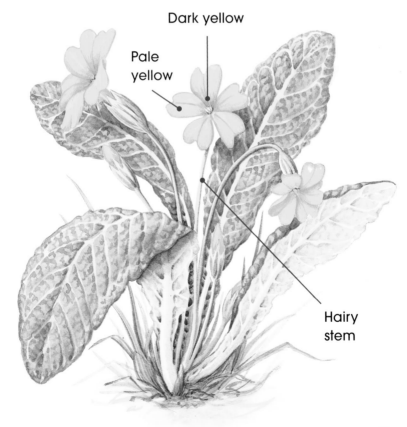

Dark yellow

Pale yellow

Hairy stem

Speedwell

Look for this blue flower in grassy places. Another name for speedwell is cat's-eye.

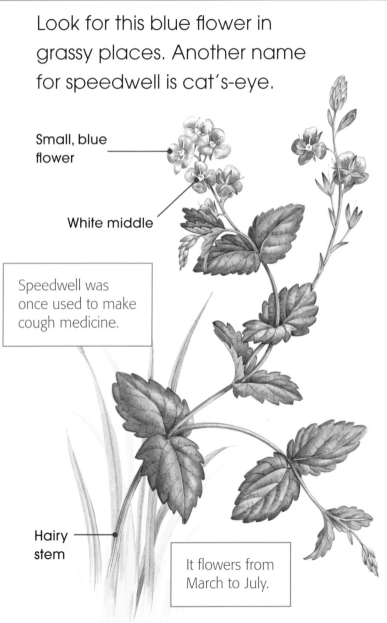

Small, blue flower

White middle

Speedwell was once used to make cough medicine.

Hairy stem

It flowers from March to July.

Bluebell

If you go to a wood or hillside in springtime, you might see lots of blue flowers. These are bluebells. They have flowers that look like tiny bells. Lots of flowers grow on one stem.

Bluebells have a strong, sweet smell.

Curled-back edge of flower

Blue flowers

Long, thin, shiny leaves

They flower from April to June.

Harebell

You can see harebells in grassy places and on cliffs and sand dunes. A harebell has blue flowers, shaped like bells. The flowers grow at the ends of long stems.

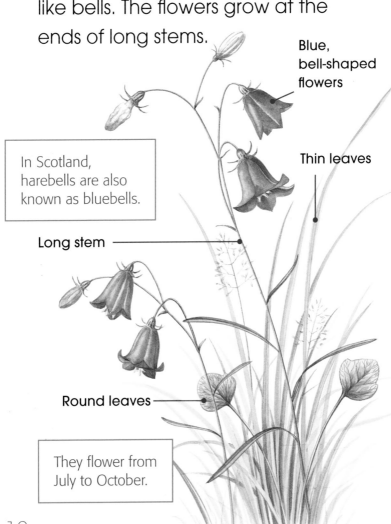

Blue, bell-shaped flowers

Thin leaves

In Scotland, harebells are also known as bluebells.

Long stem

Round leaves

They flower from July to October.

Dog rose

This is a wild rose. It has a thick stem with sharp thorns – watch out! They grow in woods, hedges and bushy areas. The flowers smell sweet.

Dog rose fruits are called rose hips. They are bright orange-red.

Look for these flowers from May to July.

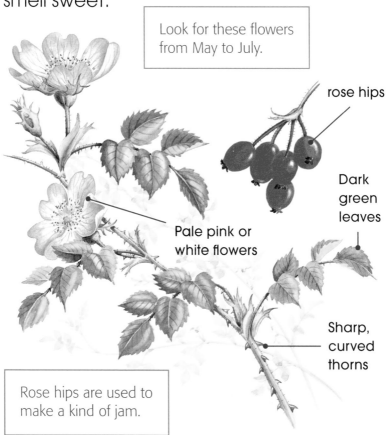

rose hips

Pale pink or white flowers

Dark green leaves

Sharp, curved thorns

Rose hips are used to make a kind of jam.

Rosebay willowherb

Rosebay willowherb grows by railways, rivers, roads and on wasteland. You can see it in gardens too. Often, you will find lots of it in one place.

Flower spike

Its seeds are light and fluffy. They blow on the breeze. Some people call them fairies.

Dark pink flowers

It flowers from June to September.

Thin pointed leaves

Heather or Ling

Look for heather on moors, bogs and heaths. It grows in clumps near the ground. When it flowers, moors turn purple.

Heather has been used to make sweeping brushes and ropes.

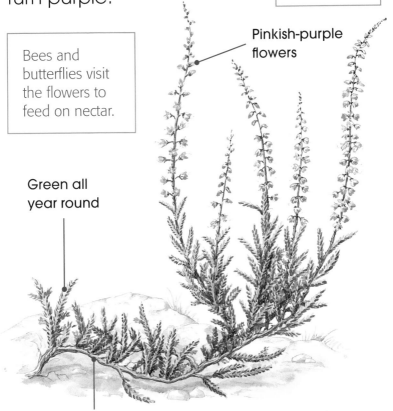

Bees and butterflies visit the flowers to feed on nectar.

Pinkish-purple flowers

Green all year round

Woody stem

It flowers from July to October.

Red campion

Red campion grows in woods, hedgerows and by roads. It often grows in groups. Red campion flowers from March to November.

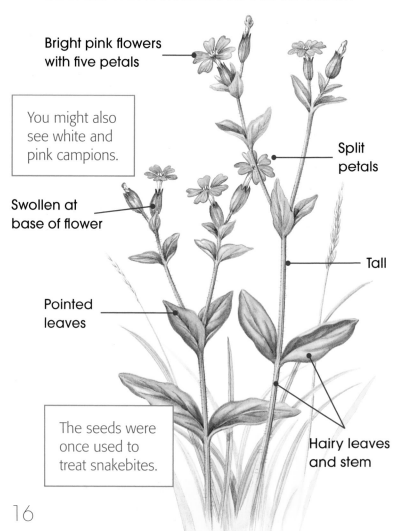

Bright pink flowers with five petals

You might also see white and pink campions.

Split petals

Swollen at base of flower

Tall

Pointed leaves

Hairy leaves and stem

The seeds were once used to treat snakebites.

16

Foxglove

Foxgloves are tall plants. They have lots of flowers on one stem. The lowest flowers open first. They flower from June to September.

Foxgloves are very poisonous.

Dark spots inside the flowers guide bees to the nectar.

Pink flowers (sometimes white)

Dark spots inside petals

Tall

Soft, furry leaves

Common vetch

Look for the curly fronds at the end of this plant's stems. They help it to climb. It lives in grassy places and hedgerows.

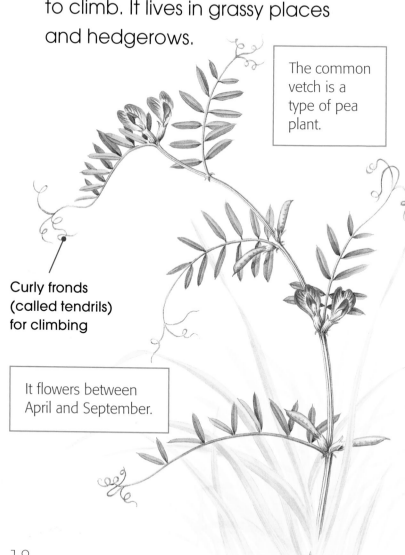

The common vetch is a type of pea plant.

Curly fronds (called tendrils) for climbing

It flowers between April and September.

Common poppy

A common poppy is easy to spot. Look for a big red flower by the side of the road, or on farmland or wasteland. You can see it from June to October.

After the petals fall off, look for the seed shakers on the end of the stems.

Bright red flower with four petals

Black (not always)

Leaves are spiky and in pairs

One poppy plant can make thousands of seeds.

Long and hairy

Snowdrop

Snowdrops bloom early in the year. Look for these white flowers from January to March in woods and hedgerows.

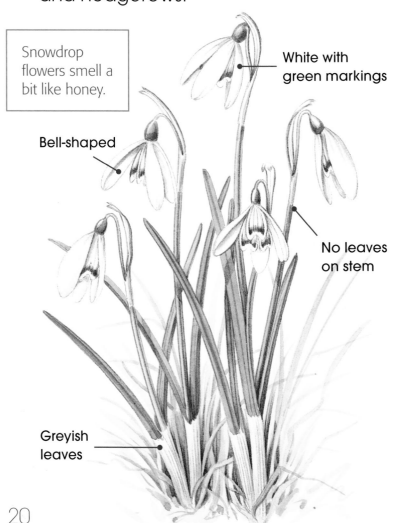

Snowdrop flowers smell a bit like honey.

White with green markings

Bell-shaped

No leaves on stem

Greyish leaves

Cow parsley

You often see cow parsley growing at the side of the road. It has lots of small, white flowers. They look a bit like umbrellas.

Cow parsley flowers from April to June.

Lots of small, white flowers

Rabbits like to eat the leaves.

Hollow stem

Fern-like leaves

21

White clover

White clover grows in gardens and at the side of the road. The flowers look like soft, white and pink balls. It flowers from May to October. Look for the heart-shaped leaves.

You might also see red clover.

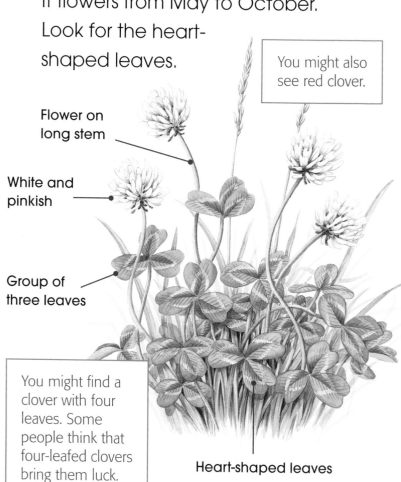

Flower on long stem

White and pinkish

Group of three leaves

You might find a clover with four leaves. Some people think that four-leafed clovers bring them luck.

Heart-shaped leaves

Common daisy

Look for daisies in short grass in gardens and parks. You can see these flowers at any time of the year. They are white with yellow middles.

Daisy flowers open in the daytime and close at night.

Their name probably comes from 'day's-eye'.

White

Yellow middle

No leaves on stem

Reddish

Leaves are on the ground

Spear thistle

A spear thistle is easy to see. It has lots of spikes – take care! It grows on wasteland and in grassy places. It flowers from July to October.

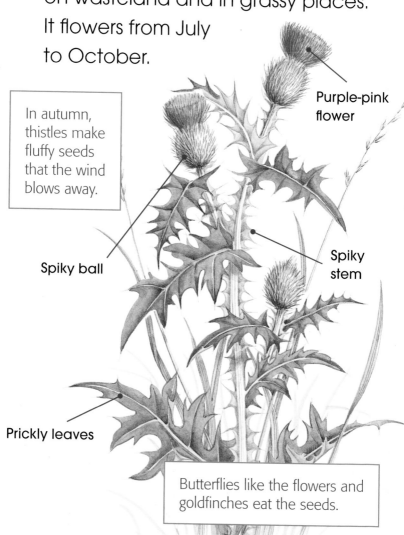

Purple-pink flower

In autumn, thistles make fluffy seeds that the wind blows away.

Spiky ball

Spiky stem

Prickly leaves

Butterflies like the flowers and goldfinches eat the seeds.

Bird's-foot trefoil

Bird's-foot trefoil is often found in grass near the sea. It trails along the ground. The seed pods on this plant look like birds' feet.

Bird's-foot trefoil flowers from May to September.

It is sometimes called bacon and eggs because of the red and yellow flowers.

Yellow flowers with some orange or red.

Trailing stem

Seed pods

Dandelion

Dandelions grow in gardens, grassy places and on wasteland. The flowers are bright yellow. The stem is hollow. If it breaks, milky juice oozes out.

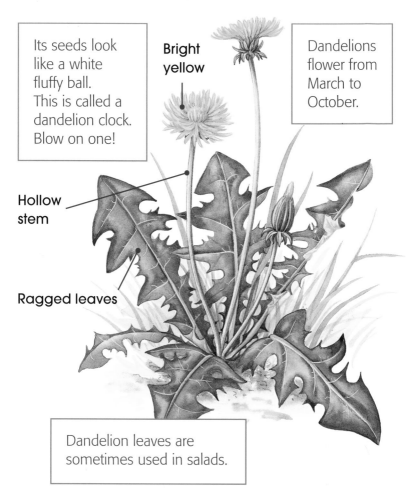

Its seeds look like a white fluffy ball.
This is called a dandelion clock.
Blow on one!

Bright yellow

Dandelions flower from March to October.

Hollow stem

Ragged leaves

Dandelion leaves are sometimes used in salads.

Thrift

Look for thrift on cliffs by the sea. It has pink flowers and narrow leaves. The leaves feel springy.

Thrift is also called the sea pink.

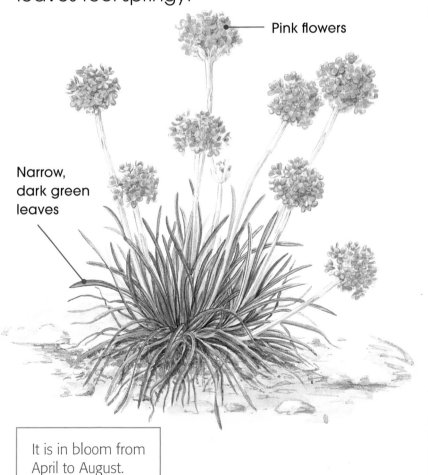

Pink flowers

Narrow, dark green leaves

It is in bloom from April to August.

Herb Robert

Herb Robert grows in shady places. You can see its small pink flowers from April to November. Its leaves and stems are often reddish.

It is also called Stinking Robert or Stinking Bob because its leaves smell horrible!

Pink flowers

Green or reddish leaves

Often reddish stem

Common mallow

The common mallow is a large plant. You can see common mallows on grassy places and wasteland. They have pink flowers.

The sticky juice from its leaves is good for bites and stings.

Pink with purple stripes

You can see its flowers from June to October.

Hairy stem

Five-pointed leaves

Cuckoo pint

This is a strange-looking plant!
Look for it in woods and hedgerows.
It flowers in April and May.

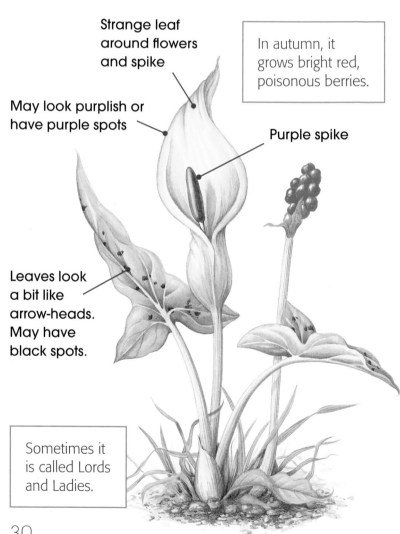

Strange leaf
around flowers
and spike

In autumn, it
grows bright red,
poisonous berries.

May look purplish or
have purple spots

Purple spike

Leaves look
a bit like
arrow-heads.
May have
black spots.

Sometimes it
is called Lords
and Ladies.

30

Teasel

This spiky plant can be taller than a man. Look for it by roads and rivers, in damp grassy places and on wasteland. The purple flowers are on a spiky cone.

Teasel flowers can be seen in July and August.

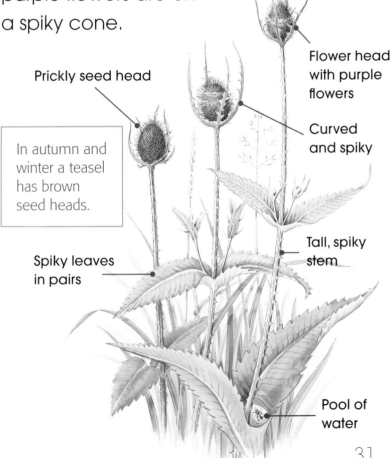

Prickly seed head

Flower head with purple flowers

Curved and spiky

In autumn and winter a teasel has brown seed heads.

Spiky leaves in pairs

Tall, spiky stem

Pool of water

31

Common dog-violet

If you go to a wood, look for common dog-violets. They are small plants with purple flowers. They are in bloom from March to June.

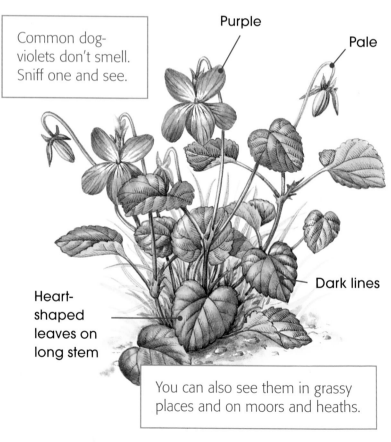

Common dog-violets don't smell. Sniff one and see.

Purple

Pale

Dark lines

Heart-shaped leaves on long stem

You can also see them in grassy places and on moors and heaths.

Stinging nettle

The stinging nettle is a hairy plant. But watch out – the hairs sting! Nettles use their stings to stop animals, such as rabbits, eating them. They flower from June to October.

Butterflies often lay their eggs on stinging nettles.

Tiny, green flowers

Hairy, pointed leaves in pairs

Some people make soup from nettles.

Hairy, flat-sided stem

Common chickweed

The common chickweed often spreads over the ground. You can see it in gardens and farm fields, and on wasteland. It has lots of tiny white flowers.

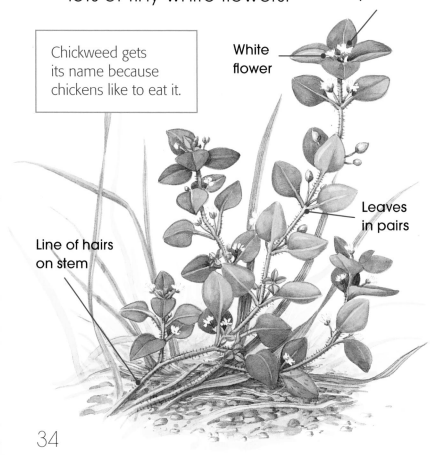

Five split petals

White flower

Chickweed gets its name because chickens like to eat it.

Leaves in pairs

Line of hairs on stem

Ox-eye daisy

This is a big daisy. It has yellow and white flowers. It grows in grassy places, woods, by roads and on wasteland. They usually grow in groups.

Ox-eye daisies are also called dog daisies or moon daisies.

White

Yellow

Leaves close to stem

They flower from May to September.

Tall stem

Great mullein

This plant is very tall and furry. It grows in grassy places, bushy places and wasteland. It has a spike of yellow flowers. The flowers can be seen from June to August.

A great mullein can be taller than a grown-up person.

Its fur helps to stop animals eating it.

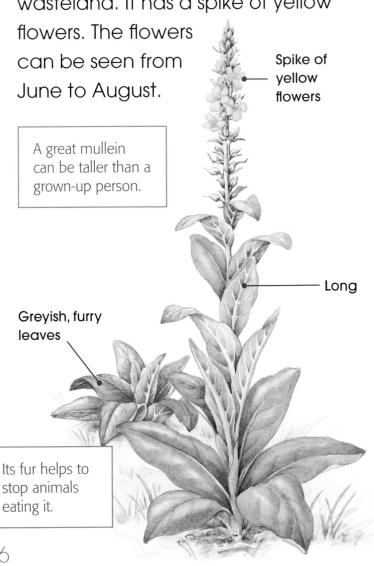

Spike of yellow flowers

Long

Greyish, furry leaves

Common hogweed

This is a big plant with big leaves and little white flowers. Common hogweed grows by roads, in grassy places and in woods. It flowers from April to November.

Common hogweed flowers have a piggy smell.

Umbrella of flowers

Big and hairy leaves

Beetles and flies feed on it.

Grooves

Hairy hollow stem

Yellow iris

These big, bright yellow flowers are found by ponds, lakes and rivers. They grow in marshes too. Look for them from May to August.

Two or three yellow flowers

Petals fold outwards

Long, pointed leaves

Thicker line down middle of leaf

Another common name for this plant is yellow flag.

Silverweed

Look on the ground for a plant with leaves that are silvery on the back. It grows on bare soil and in damp grass. You can see its yellow flowers from May to August.

People used to stuff silverweed leaves in their shoes to stop their feet aching.

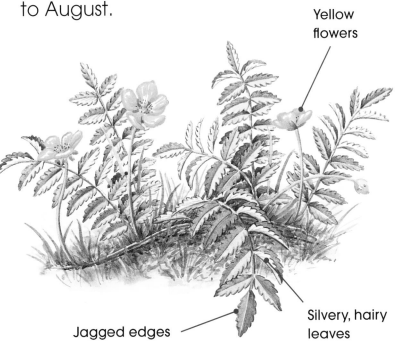

Yellow flowers

Jagged edges

Silvery, hairy leaves

Pineappleweed

Pineappleweed has strange flowers that look like tiny pineapples. It is a small plant. Look for it on paths and wasteland.

Pineappleweed flowers from May to November.

Greeny-yellow

Feathery leaves

Stems with lots of branches

It smells of pineapple too. Crush some leaves and have a sniff.

Useful words

fern a plant that doesn't flower and has feathery leaves

goldfinches small, colourful birds with bright red faces

hollow something that has an empty space inside

moors large, open pieces of land, often covered with heather

nectar the sweet liquid that flowers make to attract insects

stem the stalk of a plant

wasteland land that people once used but that nature has started to take over again

Spotter's guide

How many of these flowers have you seen? Tick them when you spot them.

Buttercup
page 6

Lesser celandine
page 7

Cowslip
page 8

Primrose
page 9

Speedwell
page 10

Bluebell
page 11

Harebell
page 12

Dog rose
page 13

Rosebay
willowherb
page 14

Heather or Ling
page 15

Red campion
page 16

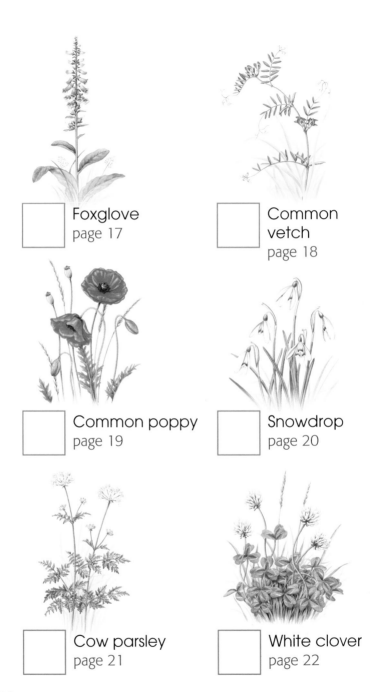

Foxglove
page 17

Common vetch
page 18

Common poppy
page 19

Snowdrop
page 20

Cow parsley
page 21

White clover
page 22

Common daisy
page 23

Spear thistle
page 24

Bird's-foot trefoil
page 25

Dandelion
page 26

Thrift
page 27

Herb Robert
page 28

45

Common mallow
page 29

Cuckoo pint
page 30

Teasel
page 31

Common
dog-violet
page 32

Stinging nettle
page 33

Common
chickweed
page 34

Ox-eye daisy
page 35

Great mullein
page 36

Common
hogweed
page 37

Yellow iris
page 38

Silverweed
page 39

Pineappleweed
page 40

Find out more

If you have enjoyed this book and would like to find out more about flowers and other wildlife, you might like RSPB Wildlife Explorers.

Visit www.rspb.org.uk/youth to find lots of things to make and do, and to play brilliant wildlife games.